Patrick Boyle

illustrations by
50s Vintage Dame

KEEP COOLIDGE AND CARRY ON
THE WISDOM OF
Jennifer Coolidge

Smith
Street
Books

CONTENTS

Introduction

She's beauty, she's grace, and the queen of screen and meme in equal measure. It's with reverence – and a barely stifled "yasss" – that we fall before her to beg for the wisdom and strength to carry on. Because she's Jennifer Coolidge and only she can show us the way.

JC has charted a career in Hollywood that remains beyond compare. Spending her early days waiting tables and hustling for dramatic roles, she joined legendary improv troupe The Groundlings in the 1990s and embraced her Goddess-given comedic gifts. Arguably, JC's breakout role came in 1999 as "Stifler's mom" in *American Pie*, popularizing (for better or worse) the concept of a MILF in our collective imaginations.

In 2000, as Sherri Ann Cabot in *Best in Show*, JC got to flex her improv muscles for all the world and kicked off a working relationship with mockumentary virtuoso Christopher Guest. The very next year, JC taught a grateful generation how to successfully execute The Bend & Snap as manicurist Paulette Bonafonté in *Legally Blonde*.

These roles have defined JC's career for the better part of the this century. Slapstick and faux ditziness became her bread and butter, firmly cementing JC's cult status as one-of-a-kind performer (slash gay icon). Then 2021 arrived: With the ubiquity of HBO's *The White Lotus*, her career ballooned into a fully fledged Coolidge-aissance. In a few short years, JC has become everyone's shared online obsession, and there's nobody more deserving of this stratospheric career glow-up.

In the pages that follow, we dive into the Jennifer Coolidge Cinematic Universe to find advice on living, laughing, and loving from our beloved queen and the characters she's embodied. When the weight of the world today – climate doomscapes, hyper partisanship, war, etc. – is getting you down, just let Jennifer Coolidge guide the way.

"I COULD HAVE F****** WRITTEN my own shows. I JUST WAITED AROUND FOR PEOPLE ... NOW YOU ALL KNOW: IT'S ALL IN YOUR HANDS. You can do it."

CHAPTER 1

Live

LIVING LIFE TO THE FULLEST TAKES CHUTZPAH. JUST LOOK AT J-COOL, WHO EXUDES THE KIND OF CONFIDENCE THAT CAN ONLY COME WITH KNOWING EXACTLY WHO YOU ARE. WE COULD ALL TAKE A LEAF FROM HER BOOK. OR, AS IT HAPPENS, THIS VERY BOOK.

Commit

In every aspect of life, commitment is key. You've got to go full carpe diem and seize every day. No one knew this better than Jennifer Coolidge in the 80s, working as a cocktail waitress (alongside Sandra Bullock, no less).

In her own words, JC was "partying a lot back in those years," and the Fourth of July was no exception. Wanting the night off, she rang her manager to call in sick. "It's Jennifer Coolidge," she (probably) breathed into the phone. "You're not going to believe this, but I was at a party last night and someone put a cigarette out in my eye."

When he demanded she still show up, JC arrived with half of her head wrapped in bandages by a real ambulance driver. This was not your average Halloween-pirate-costume eye patch, but fresh-out-of-major-surgery realness. Long after the day-after hangover subsided, JC maintained the ruse, walking around Manhattan one-eyed for weeks to keep up appearances. Now that's commitment.

Moral of the story: Nobody questions a confident and committed queen.
If they do, they better sleep with one eye open.

Improvise

Some of life's best moments happen when you go off script – Jennifer Coolidge credits her early improv training at The Groundlings as the foundation of her unforgettable performances. When the spotlight turns to you, it's all about letting your fears go, your guard down, and the chips fall as they may.

"I feel like the less I work on something," JC has said, "Or if I put too much energy into it – it's just a complete flop. But if I don't give a crap, and I don't put any judgment on or whatever, then it goes over way better."

Overthinking every tiny move we make – career-wise, money-wise, love-wise, even restaurant order-wise – only leads to second guessing. Instead, take a page from JC's book and just improvise, like she did for Sherri Ann, *Best in Show*'s iconic trophy wife. "We have so much in common," Sherri says of her husband, 44 years her senior. "We both love soup and snow peas, we love the outdoors, and talking and not talking. We could not talk or talk forever and still find things to not talk about."

Moral of the story: Try giving less of a crap.
Not everything we face is life or death.

Outside-of-the-box thinking is the one of the best shots humanity has at solving the big-ticket, planet-threatening issues of our time, like the imminent climate emergency. We need unorthodox and exciting solutions to get folks taking action.

Enter: Jennifer Coolidge. This is someone who doesn't just think outside of the box – she operates in a box-less dimension. Take her TIME100 Gala speech in which JC offered simple advice – with an unclear degree of sincerity – to a team of arctic researchers, that they enlist Doja Cat to perform on top of the world's melting glaciers. A bit like The Beatles' rooftop concert, only colder and far more meme-able.

Just imagine if the world came together to get big-ticket artists off the stage and into, say, endangered rainforests. They'd be saved in no time. When it comes to stopping your (literal or figurative) world from ending: dream big. You're limited only by your imagination. And maybe whether Doja Cat will check her DMs.

Moral of the story: The world's on fire,
but we'll never get bored.

Persuade

Who dares argue with a car mechanic quoting some wild price for a quick tire zhooshing? No one. Because they do it with authority: a learnable skill that can take you far.

It goes without saying, but Jennifer Coolidge is persuasion personified: the kind that comes with an air of "Why would I lie about *that*?" While useful in all situations, this skill is particularly critical in the day-to-day life of anyone with aspirations of grandeur.

Pre-fame, JC would make reservations over the phone at exclusive restaurants, or rock up to the hottest clubs ... in character. Her favorite guises were Eileen Ford (co-founder of Ford Modeling Agency) and Muffin Hemingway (fictional granddaughter of Ernest). Putting on a high-society drawl, JC found that her impressions could persuade even the snootiest maître d' that she deserved a table.

At the end of the day, if you can convince someone you deserve something, then you really do.

Moral of the story: With the power of persuasion
comes great responsibility. And great perks.

◁—◇————————◇—▷

"IF YOU EVER WANT
TO JOIN ME,
I'M DOWN IN
New Orleans
GETTING F****D UP
ON THE PORCH."

Stanislavski famously declared "There are no small roles, only small actors." Well, that attitude can be applied to just about any facet of life. It's all about making the most with what you've got, whether you're in the leading role or grinding away as a background actor.

Jennifer Coolidge always serves up an entire meal when she steps on screen. Whether she's delivering the hammiest parts or briefest of cameos, JC is the GOAT scene stealer. In 20 years, when we've all become accustomed to watching AI-generated content through some temporal lobe adapter, viewers may have forgotten what exactly happens in *The White Lotus*. But odds are, people will remember exactly who you're talking about when you say the name "Tanya McQuoid."

So, don't grimace next time you draw the short straw – it still works when the glass is half full.

Moral of the story: Opportunity comes
in all shapes and sizes, baby.

Sometimes, just getting out of bed is a Herculean task. It's often so tempting to just lay there for hours while someone, somewhere has already finished a triple marathon by dawn. But, in the face of life's most egregious challenges, we must find the perseverance to march on. Or at least get out of bed at a reasonable hour.

Jennifer Coolidge has persevered her entire working life. From a career that, for far too long, was rarely taken seriously, to wildly challenging on-set conditions. Who can forget Tanya McQuoid attempting to scatter her mother's ashes in the Pacific Ocean? While filming the scene, JC vomited between most takes from violent seasickness. But at no point did she let the nausea (or her co-stars' horror) stop her from delivering an award-winning performance and cementing her place as Hollywood royalty.

Moral of the story: When the boat of duty's a-rocking, you best come a-knocking.

Reflect

Looking back is a nice way to check in with yourself, from time to time, to see how far you've come – or maybe how far you have left to go.

Jennifer Coolidge is one of those public figures who's in a constant state of self-reflection. She's endearingly introspective. "Anyone that works for me," JC has said, "realizes I really have no business being where I am."

Maybe our queen meant this as self-effacement, but it contains some clear wisdom. Most people in positions of power – Hollywood producers, policymakers, and even everyday middle management types – find ways to let their power over others be known. But people like JC surprise us by just being along for the ride, unafraid to ask for help because they truly know themselves.

Moral of the story: Avoid management roles.
If you can't, get a very good assistant.

Slay is a state of mind. But how does one attain and maintain it? Annoyingly enough, it's really all about personal growth. You can start slaying at any time in your life – what matters is taking things into your own hands.

As Jennifer Coolidge points out, you can't rely on anyone else to succeed for you: "No one decides your fate." Especially not people in Hollywood. That's why JC encourages us to march to the beat of their own drum – write your own stories, dream up your own projects, and don't mold yourself to anyone's expectations. Learn who you are and create your own opportunities. You might get to a point where people offer you A-list work in places like Hawaii and Sicily, and that's what the slay life is all about, darling.

Moral of the story: Slay-ness is next to godliness,
and it's up for grabs to any masters of their own fate.

"WE SHOULDN'T
COME TO ANY
conclusions
BECAUSE I DO
THINK IT
JUST LIMITS
YOUR LIFE."

CHAPTER 2

Laugh

WHILE IT MAY SOUND GLIB, IT'S TRUE THAT LAUGHTER IS THE BEST MEDICINE. NOT TAKING LIFE'S OBSTACLES – OR YOURSELF – TOO SERIOUSLY MIGHT BE THE ONLY WAY TO MAKE IT FROM CRADLE TO GRAVE IN ONE PIECE. AND NO ONE DOES IT BETTER THAN JENNY C.

Delight

We live in a world where everyone thinks they're – *shudder* – kooky. We've been flattened by social media: Everyone is supposed to have a "thing" that makes them easily categorized. But there are still plenty of folks out there who love to delight people, day-to-day, without trying to flip each gag into clout.

Jenifer Coolidge is a person who loves things purely because they delight her. As a prime example, JC lives in a stately 1867 house in New Orleans' Lower Garden District, which she knows, for a fact, is haunted. When guests enter this wildly decorated home fit for a seance (think Pinterest maximalism and triple it), she is known to greet them with a lit candlestick in hand, just because she thinks it's creepy and funny. It just goes to show: You don't need to leave your own home to make an entrance.

Moral of the story: Make yourself laugh first. Others will follow.

Sometimes there's a big ol' chasm between what we want to do in life and what we're actually good at. This brings us to an enduring life lesson: knowing your natural talents and rolling with them. If you treat life any other way, you'll be swimming upstream for a long time, having far less fun.

Jennifer Coolidge always wanted to be a dramatic actor. She studied her craft at the American Academy of Dramatic Arts in New York City. "Meryl Streep was my hero," JC said of her mindset at the time. "I wanted to be that type of actor more than anything."

Casting directors shut that down real quick. JC was typecast as a comedic actress (if you haven't already, do yourself a favor and watch the *Seinfeld* episode "The Masseuse"). To her credit and the world's gratitude, JC embraced her new shtick and turned it into a lifelong career – making herself laugh, and our world a little brighter, every step of the way.

**Moral of the story: Do what comes naturally,
and have a laugh while you're at it.**

Dream

According to numerous motivational Pinterest accounts, the 21st-century philosopher Harry Styles once remarked: "A dream is only a dream until you decide to make it real." He wasn't wrong. You have to put your dreams out there – release them into the wild – and see what happens.

Jennifer Coolidge has let it be known that her dream role is to play a dolphin. It remains unclear if that means playing a dolphin for an off-Broadway interpretive theater production, as the voice of a Disney animated character, or straight-up LARPing. Clearly, JC has Big Dolphin Energy, so it just makes sense. Olivia Wilde has even announced that she'd help make this project happen.

There's nothing sheer grit – or James Cameron-level CGI – can't accomplish. If you have a dream, ignore the naysayers, including the basic laws of our universe: If you can dream it, you can be it.

Moral of the story: Eeeee ee éeee, eee èe.

Dissent

Rules are made to be broken. Binaries are meant to be questioned. The people who dissent from the status quo are the ones who lead the way, which goes for everything from frontline activism to the spicy world of comedy.

Jennifer Coolidge was told she had a one-of-a-kind funny bone for her impressions of all the serious (read: bad) students in her dramatic acting classes. Eventually persuaded to audition for The Groundlings, she now credits the improv group for saving her life. "You know, men are told they're funny from the beginning," JC told *The New York Times*. "Women are just supposed to be pretty and look nice and be quiet, and the more well-mannered you are, the better you'll do, and comedy's really about undoing all that."

In the undoing of these dude-centric film and television tropes, JC's career has been quietly radical. For all the slapstick she's served up, the joke has never once been on her. The same goes for anyone who decides to swim upstream, wherever the waters might be.

Moral of the story: Comedy is for everyone, not just the ubiquitous stand-up bros. Don't let anyone tell you otherwise.

"I THINK WE
HAVE TO REALLY TAKE
CARE OF OURSELVES
AND GET OUR OWN
THING GOING. AND THEN
IF A GUY COMES IN,
it's all great.
OR IF A GUY
DOESN'T COME IN,
it's all great."

Party

Taking time to celebrate big moments is a cornerstone of the human experience, as is getting lit for the hell of it. Folks have been fermenting things for this very purpose since 7,000 BCE. Since then, drinking has been the global pasttime – one which Jennifer Coolidge knows well.

JC reigned for a time as Certified Party Girl™ in both New York and LA. It was a period that helped formalize her icon status, and that proved a wild era doesn't mean you can't be a superstar. Although, it's here that reader caution is advised. During a speech at Emerson, her alma mater, JC did share some pointed wisdom: Save some partying till you're older. There'll be plenty of celebrating in each of life's decades, so plan accordingly, show up to work, and always stay hydrated.

Moral of the story: Pace yourself over the
course of an evening. And your lifetime.

Relish

Living in the moment is the secret to living a life full of lols. Yes, it all sounds a bit "YOLO," but we do – quite literally – only live once. So, we must always keep relishing the little (and absurd) things in our day.

If you're not sure where to start, there's an exercise you can complete right now, which you'll relish for the rest of your days. If it's not already in your hand, grab your phone. Then search the following four words: "Jennifer," "Coolidge," "saying," "hi." Hit the first video result.

What will follow are eight of the most beautiful seconds ever committed to film. (Or at least to a smartphone.) This cinematic masterpiece is strikingly simple: a tight crop on two burgundy pumps, immediately panning up a detailed cocktail dress. The rapid pan moves further upwards, respectfully passing the bust, and lands upon the glammed-up face of our beloved JC. She releases a tiny, breathy, and quintessentially Coolidge "Hiee." Now that's relishing the moment.

Moral of the story: Every second we get is
precious, so you better carpe that diem.

The internet is constantly falling in love with a new, relatable muse. We all remember Jennifer Lawrence's salt-of-the-earth Oscar campaign, and the moment we awoke to the realization that Pedro Pascal is, in fact, Daddy. These stars are iconic because of their relatability, clearly as surprised as anyone that they're a public figure.

For all her Hollywood glory – newfound and longstanding – Jennifer Coolidge feels hilariously relatable. She's like a mysterious aunt at a holiday lunch you're dying to know more about. If you can manage to ask her a question about life, she'll give it to you straight.

When JC scored Best Supporting Actress at the Golden Globes for her role in *The White Lotus*, she lived up to this reputation. Kicking off her speech, she almost immediately put the coveted trophy on the ground. "I can put this down, right?" she asked as the audience began to cackle. "I don't work out...I can't hold it that long."

Moral of the story: No matter how big your britches get, keep it humble. All us plebs will love you for it.

Shock

The element of surprise is a cornerstone of great comedy. Give 'em shock and awe and they might laugh just for lack of another reaction. Jennifer Coolidge is, of course, the queen of bewildering performances that are as sincere as they are shocking.

"You never know how she's going to approach a scene or how wild she's going to go," says Mike White, creator of *The White Lotus* and long-time friend of JC. "Sometimes when I'm writing, that kind of person can give me anxiety. But she's pretty unmatched as far as just somebody who can bring a new take on a line or a scene and make it hers."

So, how wild will JC go? For White's 40th birthday, she hired a man in a gorilla costume to gatecrash the party. Of course, the guerrilla guest caused a ruckus in the middle of the party, did a little dance, and scampered off. But JC was disappointed, feeling that he had missed the brief – "I thought he was going to strip!" It's for precisely this kind of monkey business that you'd want JC at your party. Or any occasion.

Moral of the story: The wild card is
everybody's favorite for a reason.

"I MEAN,
THOSE CHEESE
CONNOISSEURS ARE
SO FULL OF S---,
YOU KNOW
WHAT I MEAN?
IT WAS PROBABLY
Borden's
OR SOMETHING."

CHAPTER 3

Love

WHETHER IT'S IN ROMANCE, FRIENDSHIP, OR YOUR RELATIONSHIP WITH YOURSELF – LOVE IS THE SECRET SAUCE. GETTING VULNERABLE IS KEY TO TRUE LOVE OF ANY KIND, AND JEN C IS THE UNDISPUTED QUEEN OF VULNERABILITY. SHE KEEPS IT WILDLY REAL – AND WE LOVE HER FOR IT.

Confide

Letting down your guard with loved ones can open up all kinds of doors. Decades-long relationships can be completely reawakened by a moment of genuine vulnerability.

Jennifer Coolidge and Mike White's friendship has become the stuff of legend, which includes the duo's unlikely trip to Tanzania. Mike "had a big trip planned with a lover," JC has said. "And then the lover couldn't make it, so I got it!" Their weeks on safari were in cozy, romantic quarters, and it was the most time they'd ever spent in each other's company.

There's no hiding your problems in a tiny tent on the Serengeti. "It's just all out there," JC remembered. "Mike discovered, on this trip, that I was sort of sad I wasn't in a relationship. He saw me watching these wedding videos on my iPhone in the middle of the night." Years later, when she read the script for *The White Lotus*, JC knew that Tanya's scenes harked back to those vulnerable moments the two shared, and that Mike had written the show as a love letter to her.

**Moral of the story:
Vulnerability is so hot right now.**

Empathize

Awareness and compassion should be a prerequisite for participating in society, but this empathy should extend beyond humankind. Animal welfare is key to world peace: just ask Jennifer Coolidge.

In 2023, PETA crowned JC as their – very much real – Vegan Queen. Anyone who follows her on Instagram is well aware of her two beloved dogs, Bagpipes and Chewbacca, but followers may not know that JC is a long-time vegan and the former cover star of PETA's cruelty-free gift guide.

JC's dedication to a plant-based lifestyle includes putting her money where her mouth is. She told *The New York Times* that she had to turn down a lucrative hot dog commercial featuring the iconic line from *Legally Blonde 2*, "It makes me want a hot dog real bad!" JC would only reconsider if the megacorporation introduced a vegan hot dog. They didn't, and she turned down their beefed-up paycheck.

Moral of the story: An oldie but a goodie:
try walking a mile in someone else's paws.

Prioritize

Love is like so many aspects of life – there's work and then there's play. Work is the tough stuff: unpacking your baggage to let someone else into your life as a partner. You know, all that pesky personal growth your therapist is always harping on about? Play is just finding someone to have a bit of fun with.

"A lot of people that I know that are good looking are boring," Jennifer Coolidge has lamented. "Being really good looking is overrated... It doesn't really help anyone, in the end. It's a shallow thing. Unless you're sleeping with that person. Then it's kind of fun."

It takes some of us a lifetime to figure out the difference between someone being hot and being interesting. People can theoretically be both things, but at the time of writing there are no obvious examples available. Ridiculously hot people simply don't need to have more going on. That's why we need a seasoned professional like JC to cut through the BS and tell it to us straight.

Moral of the story: Hot people exist for a reason –
just don't get too distracted by them.

Initiate

There's a special kind of cringe reserved for working up the courage to message a random on the internet. How many hours of our lives have we spent drafting and re-drafting DMs that someone just skims over anyway?

Well, Jennifer Coolidge sparked an unlikely and beyond-iconic friendship by taking that plunge. In 2018, everyone in JC's life was sending her videos of Ariana Grande doing a pitch-perfect impression of her *Legally Blonde* character, Paulette – "I'm taking the dog, dumbass!"

"My friend," JC remembers, "Was like, 'You should DM Ariana,'" because it was such a good impression. "And I was like 'No, she's got like 260 million followers …and we will never ever get to her.' And then, I did it anyway, and then this response came back, and then the next thing you know, I was going to her house getting fit…for 'Thank U, Next.'"

Moral of the story: Just slide into their DMs. You know you want to.

"THERE'S ONE THING THAT CAN KEEP YOU FOREVER *young and sexy* ... PURE DENIAL."

Strategize

They say all is fair in love and war, and although historically that wisdom has proved dodgy, the two aren't dissimilar. Love can involve battlefield tactics, social media espionage, and even bondage. It takes a real tactician to get through to the other side standing.

Jennifer Coolidge has, by her own admission, had a life full of incredible and hilarious flings. There was one vacation in Hawaii where she had two simultaneous liaisons using the most 90s-sitcom-esque scheme possible.

"I ended up meeting these two guys that were best friends and I liked them both," JC said. "So, I told them that I had an identical twin and I dated both guys for two weeks." We can only imagine the *Mrs. Doubtfire*-level of antics that went down as JC flitted between her two twin identities (and Hawaii boyfriends). Like she said: "When you're younger you can just get away with anything."

**Moral of the story: Love schemes require planning.
If you're not up for that, maybe keep to one boyfriend at a time.**

Believe

Sometimes, things fall in our lap that are too good to be true. For those of us prone to self-sabotage, it's easy to start doubting whether we're even worthy of these strokes of luck. But when the universe knocks, you answer the door.

Jennifer Coolidge has widely shared that she initially rejected Mike White's offer to play Tanya McQuoid in *The White Lotus*. When the script arrived, "We were like six months into Covid," JC recalled. "I'd been locked up in my house in New Orleans just pigging out on these vegan pizzas...So, I was just like, 'No, I'm not doing this.'"

In the end, JC credits a close friend with calling her out on her own self-loathing holding her back. "I think this happens to actresses a lot," she said. "You sit around and b**** your whole life that you've never been given the role of your dreams, and then when it comes, you're like, 'Yeah, I can't do it. I ate a bunch of pizza.'" Lucky for us, JC overcame her self-doubt and got her ass to Hawaii.

Moral of the story: There's a time for pizza,
and there's a time for making it happen.

Exemplify

Role models come in all shapes and sizes. Not everyone can be a literal Malala, but kindness in everyday life reaps major karmic rewards. (Bonus points for not shouting it from the rooftops.)

In any interview, Jennifer Coolidge tries to laugh off the stories that reveal her softest side. She once hired an assistant who was going through a really rough time. This assistant couldn't drive – which is far from ideal in LA – so JC would always drive across the city and back to drop off her own assistant. Even when JC had a 4 am call time for a film shoot, she would pick up her assistant beforehand and encourage her to sleep in the passenger seat until the pair arrived on set.

Similar reports of JC's kindness crop up regularly. It's surely a surprise to no one that she exemplifies this kind of quiet compassion – that's just her vibe.

Moral of the story: Real talk – be the kindness
you want to see in the world.

"BEING REALLY
GOOD LOOKING IS
OVERRATED ... IT
DOESN'T REALLY HELP
PEOPLE, IN THE END.
IT'S A SHALLOW THING.
UNLESS YOU'RE SLEEPING
WITH THAT PERSON.
Then it's fun."

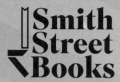

Published in 2024 by Smith Street Books
Naarm (Melbourne) | Australia
smithstreetbooks.com

ISBN: 978-1-9230-4905-5

Smith Street Books respectfully acknowledges the Wurundjeri People of the Kulin Nation, who are the Traditional Owners of the land on which we work, and we pay our respects to their Elders past and present.

Publisher: Paul McNally
Editor: Avery Hayes
Illustrations: 50s Vintage Dame
Design and layout: Stephanie Spartels
Proofreader: Ariana Klepac

Printed & bound in China by C&C Offset Printing Co., Ltd.

Book 308
10 9 8 7 6 5 4 3 2 1

This book is not affiliated with or endorsed by Jennifer Coolidge. We're just really big fans.